Trends in Southeast Asia

The **ISEAS – Yusof Ishak Institute** (formerly Institute of Southeast Asian Studies) is an autonomous organization established in 1968. It is a regional centre dedicated to the study of socio-political, security, and economic trends and developments in Southeast Asia and its wider geostrategic and economic environment. The Institute's research programmes are grouped under Regional Economic Studies (RES), Regional Strategic and Political Studies (RSPS), and Regional Social and Cultural Studies (RSCS). The Institute is also home to the ASEAN Studies Centre (ASC), the Temasek History Research Centre (THRC) and the Singapore APEC Study Centre.

ISEAS Publishing, an established academic press, has issued more than 2,000 books and journals. It is the largest scholarly publisher of research about Southeast Asia from within the region. ISEAS Publishing works with many other academic and trade publishers and distributors to disseminate important research and analyses from and about Southeast Asia to the rest of the world.

2019 no. 15

Trends in Southeast Asia

HOW WILL SHIFTS IN AMERICAN FOREIGN POLICY AFFECT SOUTHEAST ASIA?

DALJIT SINGH

Published by: ISEAS Publishing
30 Heng Mui Keng Terrace
Singapore 119614
publish@iseas.edu.sg
http://bookshop.iseas.edu.sg

© 2019 ISEAS – Yusof Ishak Institute, Singapore

All rights reserved. No part of this publication may be reproduced, stored in a retrieval system, or transmitted in any form, or by any means, electronic, mechanical, photocopying, recording or otherwise, without prior permission.

The author is wholly responsible for the views expressed in this book which do not necessarily reflect those of the publisher.

ISEAS Library Cataloguing-in-Publication Data

Names: Daljit Singh.
Title: How will shifts in American foreign policy affect Southeast Asia? / Daljit Singh.
Description: Singapore : ISEAS – Yusof Ishak Institute, November 2019. | Series: Trends in Southeast Asia, ISSN 0219-3213 ; TRS15/19 | Includes bibliographical references.
Identifiers: ISBN 9789814881333 (paperback) | ISBN 9789814881340 (pdf)
Subjects: LCSH: Geopolitics. | United States—Foreign relations. | National interest—United States. | United States—Foreign relations—Southeast Asia. | Southeast Asia—Foreign relations—United States.
Classification: LCC DS501 I59T no. 15(2019)

Typeset by Superskill Graphics Pte Ltd
Printed in Singapore by Markono Print Media Pte Ltd

FOREWORD

The economic, political, strategic and cultural dynamism in Southeast Asia has gained added relevance in recent years with the spectacular rise of giant economies in East and South Asia. This has drawn greater attention to the region and to the enhanced role it now plays in international relations and global economics.

The sustained effort made by Southeast Asian nations since 1967 towards a peaceful and gradual integration of their economies has had indubitable success, and perhaps as a consequence of this, most of these countries are undergoing deep political and social changes domestically and are constructing innovative solutions to meet new international challenges. Big Power tensions continue to be played out in the neighbourhood despite the tradition of neutrality exercised by the Association of Southeast Asian Nations (ASEAN).

The **Trends in Southeast Asia** series acts as a platform for serious analyses by selected authors who are experts in their fields. It is aimed at encouraging policymakers and scholars to contemplate the diversity and dynamism of this exciting region.

THE EDITORS

Series Chairman:
 Choi Shing Kwok

Series Editor:
 Ooi Kee Beng

Editorial Committee:
 Su-Ann Oh
 Daljit Singh
 Francis E. Hutchinson
 Benjamin Loh

How Will Shifts in American Foreign Policy Affect Southeast Asia?

By Daljit Singh

EXECUTIVE SUMMARY

- A new phase in US foreign policy, in which China is viewed as a major threat to American economic and security interests, has begun under the Trump administration.
- The strong anti-China sentiment is accompanied by efforts to "decouple" from China. If carried too far, they will alienate allies and friends whose cooperation the US will need in order to compete with China.
- In the broader American foreign policy community, there is an intense ongoing debate on how strong the push-back against China should be. Both moderates and hawks agree on the need for a "tougher" approach but differ on the degree and method of toughness. No coherent strategy has been possible partly because President Trump's thinking does not always accord with that of his own administration and partly because it is still too early in the day to come out with well-thought-out policies to support such a major change in foreign policy direction.
- The ongoing adjustments to global policy and strategy will therefore continue as the security focus shifts to the Indo-Pacific region. The "Free and Open Indo-Pacific" concept provides some signs of the broad direction policy may take but its vital economic dimension is still missing.
- There is greater recognition in Washington of the importance of Southeast Asia. Located in the middle of Indo-Pacific, it will be a contested zone between China and the US and its allies. The US will step up its public diplomacy to better promote its own narrative in Southeast Asia.

- Under the Trump administration the importance of the South China Sea to the US has risen.
- The US will remain a powerful factor in Asia despite Trump and problems at home. China is not on an inevitable path of dominance given its own significant domestic challenges.

How Will Shifts in American Foreign Policy Affect Southeast Asia?

By Daljit Singh[1]

INTRODUCTION

As China's presence and role in Southeast Asia expands, many in the region are questioning America's staying power. To explore this question, I spent a month in Washington, DC, interviewing a range of experienced experts to ascertain what the current thinking is, what the debates are, and the likely future trajectory of United States (US) policy in Southeast Asia.

This paper first addresses the present trends in US foreign policy, the mood in US policy circles towards China and the role played by President Trump, whose stances are not always in tandem with that of

---

[1] Daljit Singh is Senior Fellow and Coordinator of the Regional Strategic and Political Studies Programme at ISEAS – Yusof Ishak Institute, Singapore. This paper is based on fieldwork done in Washington, DC, in April–May 2019 as well as research undertaken in Singapore. In Washington, DC, the author interviewed sixteen long-time experts, former officials and current officials. Many of them agreed to be cited by name in this paper while a few have preferred to be cited anonymously. The author is indebted to the Sigur Center for Asian Studies of George Washington University for providing him with the opportunity to experience the stimulating intellectual climate in Washington, DC. Conversations on US foreign policy were also held with Professor Joseph C. Liow of the Nanyang Technological University, who was the first Lee Kuan Yew Chair of Southeast Asian Studies at Brookings; Andrew Thompson of the Lee Kuan Yew School of Public Policy in Singapore who is a former US Defence Department official; Malcolm Cook, Senior Fellow, ISEAS – Yusof Ishak Institute; and Dr Tim Huxley, Executive Director, IISS Asia. The author thanks them all for their time and their views. Thanks also go to John Brandon of Asia Foundation who facilitated some of the interviews.

the relevant bureaucracies and of Congress. It then goes on to examine US policy to Southeast Asia, the region's importance to US interests, the current US "influence deficiency" in Southeast Asia and the prospects of the US augmenting its influence and standing. Certain misperceptions of the US within Southeast Asia are then discussed before some concluding observations are made.

A NEW TURN IN US FOREIGN POLICY

The fundamental interest of the US in Asia has remained unchanged for over a century, since the Open Door Notes on China in 1899 and 1900. It is to keep Asia open to the US for trade and investments and to oppose closed spheres of influence. The US has used different means to ensure this—balance of power before the Pacific War, the war itself, Cold War resistance to communist expansionism, and post-Cold War primacy.

A new phase in US foreign policy seems to have begun, propelled mainly by three factors. First, the hubris and over-reach during the immediate post-Cold War period, correctly seen in hindsight as a "unipolar moment", led to wasteful and costly wars in the Middle East. Second, domestic policy failures in coping with the negative effects of globalization resulted in significant damage to US manufacturing industries and sections of the white working class. The global financial crisis of 2008–9 only accentuated the economic distress.

A reaction to these two developments was bound to come sooner or later—and it came, if rather surprisingly, in the form of candidate Trump with his "America First" rhetoric. Trump's Jacksonian ideas of self-reliance and isolationism, and the denigrating of external commitments are not new to American foreign policy. Movements advocating them have existed in many periods of US foreign policy history, particularly in the years between the two world wars.

According to Trumpism, liberal internationalism led the US to be bled and exploited by the outside world and thus, in his view, a more transactional foreign policy with American interests foremost, and more narrowly if more selfishly defined, is required. Trump is fundamentally against multilateralism and favours bilateral dealings with other countries in which America, as the more powerful player, would have advantage.

He does not speak of America's international leadership, as have most past presidents, and instead talks only about how foreign countries have exploited America and how he seeks more payment from allies and partners for the cost of US security commitments to them. Though the American security and foreign policy establishments have often not agreed with the Trumpist prescriptions, they have been unable to prevent damage to US interests by his actions such as the scrapping of the Trans-Pacific Partnership (TPP) and the callous and high-handed treatment of allies and partners.

A third major development, and perhaps the most consequential one presently shaping US foreign policy, is the rise of China. While the US was mired in Middle Eastern conflicts and the war on terrorism, China's power grew exponentially. In 2000, China's GDP was US$1.21 trillion; by 2011 it had risen to US$7.57 trillion, a sixfold increase in little more than a decade. In 2018, it was US$13.6 trillion and is expected to surpass the US economy in the early 2030s in nominal dollar terms.[2] In terms of purchasing power parity, China's economy became the world's largest in 2014. China also made rapid advances in military power which have made it more costly for the US to fight a war in the vicinity of China. These developments signal a significant decline in US strategic preponderance to which US foreign and security policies have to adjust.

It was not just the growth of China's power, but more importantly its intentions as seen by the US, which convinced US policymakers that China had emerged as a powerful strategic competitor and a threat to vital US interests. Contributing to this belief were the direction and pace of China's military modernization, complaints from the US business community about China's unfair business practices, increased repression of human rights, harassment of US surveillance ships in the South China Sea (SCS), cyberespionage of US commercial secrets and other technology thefts, the building and militarization of artificial islands in the SCS, and Beijing's contemptuous rejection of the 2016 Hague Tribunal ruling on the Philippines case relating to the SCS. After Xi

---

[2] World Development Indicators, World Bank.

Jinping's ascent to power in Beijing in 2012, it seemed clear that earlier US hopes and expectations about China had been misplaced. China was not going to be a partner of the US in preserving the existing rules-based international order; instead it seemed to seek dominance in Asia with its own regional agenda. Domestically, instead of liberalizing, China was becoming more authoritarian and repressive.

The net result was that by the end of the Obama administration, there was a widespread view in the US security and foreign policy community that policies towards China had to change and a push-back was badly needed. However this was not shared at the highest levels of the Obama administration, and the policy to sustain a cooperative relationship, "manage" the differences, and avoid tensions continued even as China became more assertive, and even aggressive. As Robert Sutter of George Washington University and a veteran observer of US policy towards Asia and US-China relations, put it:

> Obama pursued a deliberative, measured, transparent and predictable approach. He wanted to avoid tension and was reluctant to apply power. He did not want to link issues. Engagement with China was sustained on one track while on the other track China's perceived misbehaviour was "managed" to avoid tensions that would adversely affect the first track. Trump changed all this. He linked the issues, was unpredictable, did not mince his words about China, and was not afraid to create tensions. Through his words and actions, he rallied the government bureaucracies and public to stand up to China. There is now a remarkable whole of government anti-China stance which I have not seen in the last 50 years in Washington.[3]

With the change in policy towards China under the Trump Administration, the relatively benign era of US-China relations that had lasted nearly half

---

[3] Interview on 7 May 2019 in Washington, DC, with Robert Sutter, Professor of Practice of International Affairs at the Sigur Centre for Asia Studies, Elliott School of International Affairs, George Washington University.

a century and which had powered East and Southeast Asian prosperity, is now ending; and a new phase marked by deep distrust and intensified economic and strategic competition has begun.

The Mood in the US

Within the US administration and Congress, the prevalent thinking is that China seeks to oust the US from Asia and become the pre-eminent global power. Some go further to say that China constitutes an existential challenge to US economic and security well-being coupled with an ideological challenge because an increasingly powerful China will seek to foist its own authoritarian governance model and values on the world. Douglas Paal of Carnegie Endowment for International Peace observed: "We are not in a new Cold War yet, in my opinion, but there is definitely a Cold War mentality at work that may diminish both sides' capacity to manage crises effectively."[4]

Two things in particular have caused genuine alarm: first, China's advances in certain areas of high technology and its plans to become the leading technology power with its Made in China 2025 industrial policy. This is seen as a serious threat to US economic well-being and prosperity and also its military security.[5] Second is the feeling that China has infiltrated the whole US system with spies, agents of influence, cyberespionage, and influence operations. The Federal Bureau of Investigation (FBI) is publicizing what China has been doing in these areas and is going to universities to brief university administrators on the dangers. Visa applications for STEM (Science, Technology, Engineering and Mathematics) students or researchers are being more carefully screened. Chinese funding for universities and research institutes is also under scrutiny; and collaboration between US and Chinese scientific and research institutes may soon be restricted. Chinese investments in high technology are now blocked and export controls are being tightened.

---

[4] Opinion, *South China Morning Post*, 30 May 2019.

[5] It was also stressed to me by an interviewee that China is a serious challenge only in a few key technologies and the US is well ahead in the overall technology field.

In addition to the strong anti-China mood in Congress (and it is bipartisan), in the security and intelligence services, the military and the US Trade Representative's Office (USTR), a broad coalition is developing in the country. This is made up of those who lost their jobs or businesses and blame China for it; Christian conservatives; the annual Conservative Political Action Conference (CPAC) hosted by the American Conservative Union with its anti-China stance; and the Committee on Present Danger which has been revived recently to raise awareness of the danger from China with prominent members including the likes of Steve Bannon and Newt Gingrich.[6] And then there are the human rights advocacy groups incensed about the human rights situation in China, including the mass internment of Uighurs in Xinjiang province. Developments in Hong Kong are further incensing these groups as are China's pressures on Taiwan in recent years. The old Taiwan lobby is starting to make a comeback.[7] All these forces are coming together.

This anti-China sentiment had not extended as much to the American public, but recently, public opinion has been shifting. According to a Chicago Council on Global Affairs poll conducted from 22 to 24 February 2019, a majority of Americans (63 per cent) now describe the US and China as mostly rivals, up from 49 per cent who said the same in March 2018. Only one in these three (32 per cent) say the two are mostly partners, down from 50 per cent in March 2018. An August 2019 Pew poll shows 60 per cent of Americans now have an unfavourable view of China.[8]

Sentiments could move further against China once the media catches the anti-China fever.

Meanwhile, the US military is preparing for high-intensity conventional warfare with China and Russia, after having focused on low

---

[6] In its old incarnation during the Cold War, it was used to arouse awareness of the danger of communism.

[7] Much of this paragraph is from the conversation with Professor Robert Sutter.

[8] https://www.pewresearch.org/global/2019/08/13/u-s-views-of-china-turn-sharply-negative-amid-trade-tensions/.

intensity anti-terrorism for the last two decades. The defence budget has been increased and new weapons systems are being developed. Military cooperation with Japan, Australia and India has been stepped up in recent years. The trend continues, with the US wishing to collaborate more with Southeast Asian countries.

The vast US government machinery is slowly being turned around to meet the perceived challenge from China. Parallels are being drawn with the early years of the Cold War during the late 1940s when the US government bureaucracy, used to working with the Soviet Union as a wartime ally, was reoriented to deal with the Soviets as Cold War adversaries. That enterprise, and the setting up of new structures to deal with the new challenge, took nearly a decade to complete. Now the files from those days are being dusted off and revisited for ideas in the present turnaround to regard China as a strategic competitor, even an adversary, and to remove the complacency bred by nearly half a century of engagement. This will also take some years to complete, but the process has begun.[9]

Supply chains and production links have already been affected by rising wages in China and are being disrupted by the great uncertainty and distrust. The arrest of Meng Wanzhou of Huawei has added impetus to the breaking of the links. After her arrest and the subsequent arrests of two Canadians in China, personnel from US high-tech companies have become more reluctant to travel to China. The arrest of the two Canadians is regarded as a taking of hostages who have then been ill-treated in detention. This contrasts with the luxury in which Meng Wanzhou is allowed to live in Vancouver while she awaits a decision on extradition to the US. This is not helping China's image in Canada and businessmen there are now reluctant to travel to China. Such actions as well as others that are expected from the US side may also affect the sentiments of Asians who wish to invest in China. Controls on exports to China, which will be a sensitive issue for US companies that derive significant profits from the Chinese market, are likely to be further tightened in the future.

---

[9] The information in this paragraph is based on a discussion with a former senior US defence official who is presently involved in this "turnaround" task.

All my interviewees described the strategic competition with China as "indefinite", "multi-decade" or "very long term", and as one that will continue well beyond the Trump administration.[10] One senior official of the first Obama administration who personally believes in both a US push-back against China as well as engagement in some areas said: "The present course has been set irreversibly for future administrations. Change will be very difficult."[11]

In the midst of the hawkish thinking and policies within the US administration, an intense debate on China and US policy to China is going on in the broader US foreign policy community comprising primarily former officials and scholars in think-tanks and universities.[12] Members of the previous administration are very much on the defensive and are made to feel that they had allowed all this to happen and not taken action. Over a hundred of them recently published an "Open Letter" criticizing the Trump Administration for unnecessarily damaging US-China relations.[13] While a broadly agreed upon new consensus has yet to emerge, and the China policy debates in Washington and across the foreign policy community nationally remain contested and divisive, there has been an evident and widely shared shift towards advocating

---

[10] Martin Wolf of the *Financial Times* entitled a comment in the 11 August 2019 edition of the newspaper as "The Looming 100-year US-China Conflict". He noted: "Across the board rivalry with China is becoming an organizing principle of US economic, foreign and security policies." Wolf was struck by the zero-sum attitude towards China among American participants at the 2019 Bilderberg conference.

[11] Interview in Washington, DC, 8 May 2019.

[12] For summaries of the evolving debate, see Gilbert Rozman, "The Debate on China Policy Heats Up: Doves, Hawks, Superhawks, and the Viability of the Think Tank Middle Ground", *The Asan Forum*, 16 July 2019, http://www.theasanforum.org/the-debate-over-us-policy-toward-china-heats-up-doves-hawks-superhawks-and-the-viability-of-the-think-tank-middle-ground/.

[13] M. Taylor Fravel et al., "China Is Not an Enemy", *Washington Post*, 3 July 2019.

a "tougher" and more "competitive" strategy.[14] In a recent task force report, one group of specialists and former officials sought out a less confrontational and more middle ground of "smart competition".[15]

Among the very few who do not advocate a tougher stance against China is Michael Swaine of the Carnegie Endowment for International Peace. He does not believe that China at this stage has decided to displace the US and create a Sinocentric Asia, and, contrary to what many others think, he sees China's actions as defensive and meant to safeguard its own security. He said:

> China now is scared that the US has adopted a hard line and will seek to undermine China. In the US today even moderates like former Defence Secretary Mattis want to get along with China from a position of US dominance. The US has a dominance-oriented mind. China is expanding its power and influence abroad while managing stability at home, not an easy task in view of the many stresses from abroad in an era of globalization ... Xi Jinping is resorting to hard authoritarianism to keep stability at home as China navigates the twenty-first century economy with dangers of a "colour revolution". Ultimately, this will be a failed strategy for many reasons, but it is China's way of maintaining control. The demonizing of China should stop ... We need to compete effectively with China, not mount a crusade.[16]

---

[14] See, for example, Aaron Friedberg, "Competing with China", *Survival* 60, no. 3 (2018); Robert D. Blackwill and Ashley J. Tellis, "Revising U.S. Grand Strategy Towards China", Council on Foreign Relations Special Report No. 72, March 2015, http://carnegieendowment.org/files/Tellis_Blackwill.pdf; Nikki Haley, "How to Win Against Beijing: Getting Tough on Trade Is Just the First Step Toward Countering China", *Foreign Affairs*, 18 July 2019, https://www.foreignaffairs.com/articles/china/2019-07-18/how-confront-advancing-threat-china.

[15] Orville Schell and Susan L. Shirk, eds., "Course Correction: Toward an Effective and Sustainable China Policy", February 2019, https://asiasociety.org/sites/default/files/inline-files/CourseCorrection_FINAL_2.7.19_1.pdf.

[16] Interview with Michael Swaine, Senior Associate at Carnegie Endowment for International Peace, Washington, DC, on 29 April 2019.

The Trump Factor[17]

Trump dislikes anything that constrains him, so he does not want to be bound by the institutional process within government. The inter-agency meetings of previous administrations are not functioning. In normal times, such meetings take place a number of times a week, enabling people of different departments to talk to each other, forge consensus and unify policy. Under Trump, officials often try to work around this problem by arranging de facto inter-agency meetings quietly among themselves, while each agency sometimes acts on its own.[18]

Trump hovers above the anti-China attitude in the bureaucracies and Congress and has at times actually been a restraint on it, at least tactically, because his approach to China has often seemed transactional and related to his perceived domestic political needs. But, because he is time and again not on the same wavelength with his officials on strategic and security issues and because of his capriciousness and unpredictability, and his lack of an in-depth understanding of issues, he introduces great uncertainty into the US foreign policy equation.

According to one senior think-tank scholar, an example of Trump's modus operandi was the first summit with Kim Jong-un in Singapore:

> He was given background and strategy papers to prepare him for the summit. He did not read them, confident of his own ability to make a deal. Being so unprepared, he accepted Kim's definition of the issue which was to create a peace regime first, then improve relations and finally denuclearize. This was just the reverse of what the briefing papers had defined the issue for him. Part of the problem was his one-to-one meeting with Kim, with no notes taken. At this meeting he committed himself to a peace deal and nobody in the US government at first knew this. Once the policy

---

[17] The information in this section was derived from conversations with a number of think-tank scholars in Washington, DC, during April–May 2019.

[18] Interview with a think-tank scholar in Washington, DC, 2 May 2019.

team got to know of it they pulled themselves together—Bolton, Pompeo and others—and were able to intervene. Generally, the officials including his senior security and foreign policy advisers are terrified of his one-to-one meetings with Xi, Putin and Kim. After the first one-to-one summit with Kim, officials got to know of what transpired from the interpreter's notes. But subsequently Trump made sure that they could not get the interpreter's notes.[19]

Trump does give officials in the security and trade apparatus considerable leeway. In this sense the situation is very different from the Obama administration when every important move or at times even not-so-important ones had to be cleared with the president lest it upset China. Military commanders, for example the Indo-Pacific commander, now have much more freedom of action in operational matters than before (such as freedom of navigation operations in the South China Sea).

However Trump owes these officials no loyalty and they have to be concerned about his intervention in areas or subjects important to him. For example, on Taiwan, Trump was concerned that officials may go too far to strengthen ties with Taiwan because apparently he had an understanding with Xi Jinping to respect China's sensitivity over Taiwan on the assumption that Xi would help him on North Korea. Trump removed one official for exceeding what he considered was prudent in dealings with Taiwan and he also personally vetted the level of American attendance at the opening of the new American Institute Taiwan (AIT) building in Taipei.[20]

Trump has done real damage to US interests through his unilateralism and by treating allies and partners shabbily. How much more damage will he do to other important US interests like America's key Asian alliances? When asked this, my respondents generally felt alliances in the Asia-

---

[19] Interview with the same think-tank scholar, 2 May 2019.

[20] I was told by the same interviewee that Trump had also instructed the then National Security Adviser, John Bolton, an anti-China hawk, not to speak publicly on Taiwan.

Pacific region have survived and will probably continue to survive. But what if Trump is elected for another term? According to Ashley Tellis, "Trump has done a lot of damage, but he cannot destroy the system. The scaffolding will still be there. Still, he will be very negative for US foreign policy if he is re-elected because then there will be fewer restraints on him."[21] Others seem less concerned. While acknowledging that he will remain a wild card, they felt that the people he will appoint to key posts in a second Trump administration will almost certainly be hawkish conservatives or military types whom he would listen to.

On China, there is a view that Trump is interested only in the economic side of the relationship and the domestic political benefits he can derive from it. However, this may be a superficial interpretation. According to Marvin C. Ott of the Woodrow Wilson Center: "Pushing back against China is central to Trump's foreign policy. He may be transactional with other countries, but not with China. He is convinced that China is out to harm the US and his concern about China is echoed throughout the Administration."[22] This view is shared by Joseph Liow who also said that pushing back against China is central to Trump's foreign policy.[23] Developments since earlier 2019 when these interviews were conducted lend some credence to this interpretation.

It was too early in May 2019 to discuss the 2020 presidential election, but I did ask two of my distinguished interviewees whether Joe Biden, then the Democratic front runner, would maintain the current hardline stance on China if he became president. They felt that by instinct Biden would be more moderate on China. There was a whiff of concern among my respondents that he might be be too soft. He had spoken against

---

[21] Interview with Ashley Tellis, Tata Chair for Strategic Affairs and Senior Fellow at the Carnegie Endowment for International Peace, 24 April 2019.

[22] Interview with Marvin C. Ott, 16 May 2019. He is Visiting Professor, Johns Hopkins University; Senior Scholar, Woodrow Wilson International Center; and a former Professor of National Security Policy at the National War College.

[23] Interview in Singapore, 4 March 2019. Professor Joseph C. Liow is Dean, College of Humanities, Arts and Social Sciences, Nanyang Technological University, Singapore.

"anti-China hysteria" during the Obama administration, and made one early reference on the campaign trail that China was not a competitor of the US. One respondent thought that because of his age, Biden may be finding it difficult to adjust to the new realities. But in the end, both felt that because of the great change of thinking within the government, Biden will have no choice but to adjust. There may be a change in style and approach and a measure of moderation in certain areas, but the basic thrust of the policy of push-back against China will remain.

Policy Coherence and Strategy

Given Trump's worldview, his working style and the lack of inter-agency coordination, it is not surprising that the overall approach to China and other policy issues lacks coherence, and in fact appears erratic.

Hawks in the defence, security, intelligence and trade bureaucracies seeking full-spectrum, all-of-government push-back tend to look at the outside world through the prism of US-China relations.[24] For example, Secretary of State Pompeo, even when visiting Europe and Latin America goes on anti-China tirades, and Vice-President Pence is no different. At present, they seem to be having a strong influence on policy. Further, as Douglas Paal of the Carnegie Endowment for International Peace describes it, younger and younger people have filled posts in various departments, many of whom do not have a deep understanding of the issues or of the history of US policy, and thus are prone to acting unwisely. He observes: "Across the board, responsible American officials have lost patience with and understanding for China. When combined with a vainglorious and shallow leader and his chorus, it is a dangerous combination."[25]

---

[24] See Robert Sutter, "Washington's 'Whole-of-Government' Pushback Against Chinese Challenges: Implications and Outlook", *Pacnet*, no. 26 (2019), https://www.pacforum.org/analysis/pacnet-26---washingtons-whole-government-pushback-against-chinese-challenges—implications.

[25] See *South China Morning Post*, 10 October 2018.

The tendency among the hawks in the bureaucracies is to strike back against China irrespective of the collateral damage to other countries, including friends of the US. But others, especially in think-tanks, realize that this kind of approach is counter-productive and changes will need to be made. Michael Green in CSIS, when asked whether this approach will be successful said:

> The way they are doing it now, it will not succeed or be sustained. It undermines allies and friends. There is a need to calibrate the push-back with other US interests, both domestic and international, such as interests of farmers in the US and interests of allies, friends and multilateralism. Even Japan is not standing up for a trade war with China.[26]

He felt that adjustments will eventually have be made, arguing that historically it has taken time for the US to adjust to a major strategic change and challenge. Initially it has tended to overreact, but after some time the pieces of policy fall together and a more sensible strategy is shaped.

Kurt Campbell similarly said:

> There is a lot of lack of understanding among people running the present strategy. The US has to engage in some areas and compete in other areas with China. The US must realize that it may not be possible to continue with its hegemony and should instead seek to achieve a balance of power. China on the other hand must realize that US-China relations are not a zero-sum game.[27]

---

[26] Interview in Washington, DC, 7 May 2019. Michael J. Green is Senior Vice-President for Asia and Japan Chair at CSIS, Washington, DC. He was senior director for Asian affairs in the National Security Council under President George W. Bush.

[27] Interview in Washington, DC, 8 May 2019. Kurt M. Campbell is Chair and CEO of the Asia Group. He was US Assistant Secretary for East Asian and Pacific Affairs from 2009 to 2013. See also Kurt M. Campbell and Jake Sullivan, "How America Can Both Challenge and Co-exist with China", *Foreign Affairs*, September/October 2019.

There are those in policy circles who would want comprehensive economic "decoupling" from China. However, as Ashley Tellis puts it:

> Those who advocate cutting all US economic ties to China are like King Canute trying to turn the tide. It cannot be done. You cannot destroy globalization, short of war. But supply chains in some sectors can be changed, for example in the defence sector—you don't get components and supplies from China.[28]

Hank Paulson, former US Secretary of the Treasury, in a speech given at the Bloomberg Forum in Singapore on 6 November 2018, addressed the dangers of a comprehensive decoupling: "It would result in the erection of an Economic Iron Curtain that closes large parts of the global economy to the free flow of trade and investment and impede innovation". "Decoupling", he said, "is easier when you are actually a couple, but this is not the case because many other countries are involved in trading and investing with China. These countries will not follow the US in restricting the flow of goods, technology capital and people to China. So in its efforts to isolate China, the US risks isolating itself."[29]

It would be more realistic to have partial decoupling in critical industries related to American military and national security needs. Yet, decoupling is proceeding even as the debates rage. The Commerce Department in the US has added more companies to its black list (the Entity List) and such actions are expected to continue. The range of Chinese products under suspicion on national security grounds also keeps widening, and it is not known where it will stop.[30] Also being contemplated are restrictions on

---

[28] Interview with Ashley Tellis, 24 April 2019.

[29] See Edna Curran, "Paulson Warns of 'Economic Iron Curtain' Between US, China", Bloomberg, 6 November 2018, https://www.bloomberg.com/news/articles/2018-11-07/paulson-warns-of-economic-iron-curtain-between-u-s-china.

[30] See Edward Luce, "Trump Is Serious about US Divorce from China", *Straits Times* (Singapore), 21 September 2019, p. A38; Anna Swanson, "US Fear of 'Spy Trains' May Block China Cars", *New York Times* (International edition), 16 September 2019, p. I.

Chinese access to US capital markets, including the delisting of Chinese companies from American stock exchanges.

On the geopolitical front, the broad direction the US is heading towards is expressed in its Free and Open Indo-Pacific (FOIP) concept. Embodied in it are all the important principles that the US has sought to adhere to in its Asia policy for more than a century: openness of Asia to all powers for commerce, free and fair trade, freedom of navigation and overflight, and a rules-based international order.

However, beyond the principles, the FOIP will need more substance. For a start, it can be seen as an extension of Obama's pivot or rebalance policy. Michael Green sees the FOIP as being based on the traditional Mahanian view of Asian strategy of offshore power projection and close ties with Japan and like-minded countries. While supportive of it, he felt it was still too narrow, relying mostly on Japan while ignoring Southeast Asia. He said: "It is crucial to bring in others for diplomatic and economic strategies while the US provides the military muscle. Japan and Australia are doing a very good job in pushing for this in Washington and elsewhere."[31]

The FOIP has yet to marshal an economic response to crucial dimensions of the China challenge, namely economic and infrastructural. The US government is not in the infrastructure building business; that remains the responsibility of the private sector. Some initial steps have been taken to try to remedy this shortcoming—such as the BUILD (Better Utilization of Investment Related to Development) Act. However, it is still unclear how these will work out (see discussion below).

While the economic dimension may take time to jell, it would be a mistake to dismiss the FOIP as just a shell or skeleton without any flesh.[32] A careful look reveals much that has been going on informally and below the radar. For instance, a military dimension already exists in the form of the Quad. Military forces of the Quad countries have been training

---

[31] Michael Green interview, 7 May 2019.

[32] U.S. Department of Defence Indo-Pacific Strategy Report, June 2019, https://media.defense.gov/2019/Jul/01/2002152311/-1/-1/1/DEPARTMENT-OF-DEFENSE-INDO-PACIFIC-STRATEGY-REPORT-2019.PDF.

together bilaterally or trilaterally and have acquired interoperability in coming together in a crisis. James Przystup of the National Defence University in Washington, DC, described the FOIP as follows:

> At present, it is like pieces of a jigsaw puzzle moving around: US alliances, TPP 11 multilateralism. [Pence has also supported ASEAN multilateralism.] British and French naval moves in South China Sea; evolution of the US alliance structure like minilaterals even without the US; the Quad; and India. Eventually these floating pieces will come closer together. With more co-ordination there will be more leverage.[33]

Meanwhile the decline of America's relative strategic and economic power is bound to be reflected in adjustments to its global policy and strategy. This has in fact been apparent since the Obama administration's unwillingness to get involved in the Syrian conflict, and since its calls for "burden sharing" and more partnerships. The tendency towards retrenchment has continued under the Trump administration, with officials seeking to review foreign involvement with the question "what is in it for us?" and seeking ways out of the conflicts in the Middle East and Afghanistan as the country tries to focus on the Indo-Pacific region.

American primacy after World War II was a historical anomaly brought about by the very special circumstances of the post-war world. For many years before World War II, the US relied on a balance of power to secure its interests in Asia, often in a multipolar geopolitical setting. This is likely to be the direction in the future. Whatever form a balance-of-power strategy will take in the Indo-Pacific, alliances, partnerships and "burden sharing" will be constituting elements in it.

THE US AND SOUTHEAST ASIA

What are the implications for Southeast Asia of this mega-shift in American thinking and policy towards China?

---

[33] Interview with James J Przystup, Centre for Strategic Research, Institute for National Strategic Studies, National Defence University, 3 May 2019.

Under the Obama Administration

President Obama's response to China's assertiveness was his pivot or "rebalance" to Asia, which prominently included Southeast Asia. It entailed a number of policy moves:

- Enhanced multilateral and bilateral diplomacy with ASEAN and Southeast Asia, with the president meeting ASEAN leaders at summits, even as robust exchanges in educational, scientific and other fields continued.
- Continuation of the strong defence diplomacy that the Defence Department maintains with the militaries of key Southeast Asian countries and the stepping up of capacity building of allies and partners, especially in the maritime domain, through exercises, sale of equipment and training.
- Improving the US military's access to the region. The US no longer enjoyed local military hegemony in Southeast Asia as it did in the 1960s and 1970s when it had significant military assets in Thailand and the Philippines. Military assets had to be brought to Southeast Asia from elsewhere, giving rise to issues of access and logistics. The Enhanced Defence Cooperation Agreement (EDCA) with the Philippines signed in 2014 provided access to a number of Philippines military bases for the US armed forces. An enhanced Defence Cooperation Agreement (DCA) was signed with Singapore in December 2015. It was during the Obama administration that US Littoral Combat Ships and the P-8 Poseidon maritime surveillance and anti-submarine aircraft began operating out of Singapore. Malaysian Prime Minister Najib Razak granted American reconnaissance aircraft access to airfields in East Malaysia.
- Finally, President Obama recognized the critical importance of economic engagement and had a clear economic prong to his pivot to Asia, including Southeast Asia, in the form of the TPP. However, he flunked it by not acting fast enough to get it through Congress.

These were all generally considered good moves by the stakeholders. However, President Obama's biggest weakness was the lack of will in using US power to check Chinese advances in the South China Sea. No red lines were drawn, and the Chinese were able to take advantage of that.[34]

Under the Trump Administration

While President Obama gave increased attention to ASEAN, the Trump administration has given the region less consideration. Obama's stance, to be sure, was an aberration in US-ASEAN relations in the post-Vietnam War history. Thus, another way to look at the change today may be to regard it as a return to normal.[35] In the first year of his administration, President Trump received a few Southeast Asian leaders in the White House and talked to a few on the phone. He was present at the ASEAN summit in Manila in 2017. Although all this was on the urging of officials, it nevertheless raised hope in Southeast Asia that there would not be much of a departure from the previous administration. The degree of summit-level attention decreased thereafter, however, even if senior officials, including the Secretary of State and the Secretary of Defence, have continued to attend ASEAN meetings and have expressed support for ASEAN and ASEAN centrality.[36] In 2008, President Trump

---

[34] For a Leninist state well-versed in the power game, this must have been a surprising gift. A senior Chinese scholar with connections to the Chinese authorities described President Obama as a "dreamer" in a private conversation in Singapore in 2016. Wrong signals were sent in leaked reports that the US would not go to war with China over "rocks in the South China Sea". Bonnie Glaser of CSIS, in a discussion in Singapore in January 2019 noted that China desisted from reclamation at Scarborough Shoal after Obama warned President Xi in April 2016 of "very severe consequences" if China proceeded to do so, suggesting that the outcome in the SCS might have been different if handled differently from the start.

[35] Joseph Liow describes US engagement with Southeast Asia after the Cold War as "episodic". See Joseph Chinyong Liow, *Ambivalent Engagement: The United States and Regional Security in Southeast Asia After the Cold War* (Washington, DC: Brookings Institution Press, 2017).

[36] A recent reiteration of this was made by Secretary of State Mike Pompeo at the ASEAN Ministerial Meeting in Bangkok (29 July – 3 August 2019). He also expressed support for the ASEAN Outlook on the Indo-Pacific.

had discussions with Singapore Prime Minister Lee Hsien Loong when he visited Singapore for his summit meeting with Kim Jong-un. Yet, as Satu Limaye observed: "The present administration acknowledges the centrality of ASEAN amidst the backdrop of less interest in multilateralism. But, acknowledgment is not the same as utilization and I think we can do more to work with ASEAN".[37]

Among officials and most knowledgeable experts, there are considerable frustrations with ASEAN's lack of coherence and unity, especially with regard to the SCS. For example, it was damning that ASEAN could not even come together to support The Hague ruling on the Philippines case against China on the SCS, i.e., to support a ruling of international law. However, despite these issues, there is a growing recognition of the importance of Southeast Asia in the geopolitical contest with China.[38]

How Important Is Southeast Asia to the US?

Northeast Asia has traditionally been much more important to the US than Southeast Asia. It is the part of Asia where the US has a staunch ally, Japan, which is the world's third largest economy and which provides bases for forward deployment of US military forces. Northeast Asia is also the place where the US could possibly become involved in a major power war over Korea or Taiwan (though now this could also happen in the SCS where the navies of China and the US and its allies are operating at close quarters in a contested sea). There are no strong or reliable allies in Southeast Asia capable of military "burden sharing" with the US. Furthermore, the volume of US trade with Northeast Asia

---

[37] Interview, 9 May 2019 at East-West Center, Washington, DC. Satu Limaye is Vice-President and Executive Director, East-West Center, Washington, DC.

[38] It was remarked to me by a former senior official, now a think-tank scholar, that Southeast Asian embassies in Washington, apart from the Singapore Embassy, have not been very good in putting across the Southeast Asian/ASEAN case to American audiences and policymakers. However, Japan and Australia have done a good job in putting forward the importance of Southeast Asia.

has always surpassed that with Southeast Asia. While US investments in Southeast Asia are larger than those it has in Northeast Asia, the latter are nonetheless far from negligible.

To be sure, despite frustrations with Southeast Asia—lack of ASEAN unity, lack of reliable allies, authoritarian governments and human rights violations (governance and human rights issues remain important to the US Congress)—there seems to be growing recognition of the greater strategic and economic importance of this subregion of Asia, perhaps greater than at any time since the Vietnam War in the 1960s–1970s. Michael Green has argued that:

> Southeast Asia and the Korean Peninsula can no longer be considered strategically important only because they form the frontlines against the hegemonic aspirations of America's adversaries. Korea is the world's twelfth largest economy, and ASEAN as a whole constitutes America's fifth largest trading partner. These states must today be viewed as essential "strong points" in the same way Kennan saw Germany and Japan in his early concepts of containment.[39]

David Shambaugh of George Washington University also sees Southeast Asia becoming "an epicentre" of escalating US-China competition and Southeast Asian countries likely "becoming increasing *objects* of this competition".[40]

Strategically, Southeast Asia juts out like a wedge from the mainland of Asia towards Australia, dividing the Indo-Pacific region into a Pacific Ocean side and an Indian Ocean side. So no Indo-Pacific strategy will work without taking Southeast Asia and ASEAN into account. And this

---

[39] See Michael J. Green, *By More than Providence: Grand Strategy and American Power in the Asia Pacific since 1783* (New York: Columbia University Press, 2017), p. 546.

[40] David Shambaugh, "US-China Rivalry in Southeast Asia: Power Shift or Competitive Coexistence?", *International Security* 42, no. 4 (Spring 2018).

wedge is intersected by several narrow straits through which commerce, including oil which is so important to the economies of Northeast Asia and the navies of the major powers passes, endowing great strategic importance to maritime Southeast Asia and especially Indonesia.

Southeast Asia had a total stock of US$329 billion in US investments in 2018, which is more than the investments from China, Japan, India and South Korea combined.[41] These have been increasing by an average annual rate of 10 per cent over the past decade. US exports to Southeast Asia presently support over half a million US jobs. Southeast Asia's economy, encouraged by favourable demographics, is expected to grow by an average of 5.5 per cent a year, to become the fourth largest economy in the world by 2050. The region's middle class is expected to double from 135 million to 334 million by 2030 (51 per cent of the population).[42] For these reasons, Alex Feldman, CEO of US-ASEAN Business Council, is bullish on Southeast Asia, arguing that it is the place to be for investors.[43] With the ongoing trend to reduce supply chain links with China or at least to diversify to avoid overdependence on it, Southeast Asia has the opportunity to take advantage of the situation if the ASEAN member states manage to expedite regulatory and other reforms to improve their investment climate.[44]

---

[41] A large portion of US investment in Southeast Asia goes to Singapore where it supports "hundreds of thousands" of jobs, according to Singapore Prime Minister Lee Hsien Loong; part of it is reinvested from Singapore to other Southeast Asian countries as Singapore investments. According to Alex Feldman, CEO of US-ASEAN Business Council, after Singapore, Thailand is the second largest recipient of US investment, with Malaysia in third place. US investment in Vietnam is increasing rapidly.

[42] The statistics in this paragraph are from East-West Centre's *ASEAN Matters for America, America Matters for ASEAN* (2019) and US-ASEAN Business Council.

[43] Conversation with Alex Feldman in Washington, DC, 23 May 2019.

[44] More than one of my interlocutors said that ASEAN and Southeast Asian countries need to come out quickly with such reforms. One suggested an ASEAN-wide investment treaty for this purpose.

A very important reason why the US cannot afford to neglect Southeast Asia is that it and the sea routes through it are critical to America's most important Asian ally, Japan.[45] The danger is that if the US were to abandon Southeast Asia, Japan could become unnerved enough to reach an accommodation with China. Such an eventuality would undermine the US position in Asia as Japan provides the bases for the forward deployment of US military forces.

An emergence of a closed Chinese sphere of influence embracing Southeast Asia would be inimical to the fundamental US commercial and strategic interest of keeping the Indo-Pacific region open to all states. This is an increasing concern in Washington as China increases its presence and interactions with Southeast Asian states and societies.

What Resources Can the US Commit to Southeast Asia?

While the importance of Southeast Asia is perceived to be increasing, the gap between President Trump's priorities and interests and those of the national security community persists. There is also the gap between what is being said about China (and Southeast Asia) and the level of resources, including attention, that the administration is willing to commit to Southeast Asia This will depend on whether the administration follows Vice-President Pence's idea of a full-spectrum competition with China or a more moderate strategy. This matter remains unsettled as the administration remains preoccupied with issues in Northeast Asia and the Middle East. A senior think-tank scholar described the present policy to Southeast Asia as "muddling along". However, beyond resources and strategy, as one interviewee pointed out, an important factor would be how much local and allied support the US can muster.

One important challenge for the US is to provide countries with the option of an alternative to China's infrastructure projects under the Belt

---

[45] The US itself is now self-sufficient in oil and it can possibly bypass the sea routes through Southeast Asia.

and Road Initiative (BRI). The BRI is much more than an infrastructure or economic initiative. Packed into it are levers of political influence and strategic advantage over a large swathe of the Indo-Pacific. The Maritime Silk Road is, in fact, a Chinese Indo-Pacific strategy. The US and its allies recognize the broad challenge posed by the BRI and the need to compete more effectively with it. The US government cannot match China in dollar-to-dollar investments in Southeast Asia for infrastructure construction, which in any case can be done only by the US private sector. So it is likely to try to work more with the private sector and with like-minded countries to focus on investments that can help Southeast Asia, and make a difference to American standing in Southeast Asia.

Some initial steps in that direction have in fact been taken. In October 2018, President Trump signed into law the United States BUILD Act and the agency set up under it, the United States Development Finance Corporation (USDFC), became operational on 1 October 2019. USDFC will double US development finance capacity to US$60 billion for infrastructure projects on a sustainable public-private partnership, possibly also with the participation of allies like Japan and Australia.[46] The USDFC may liaise closely with the State Department and the security agencies to strengthen the American response to the BRI through infrastructure development. When properly staffed and resourced, it should have the potential to compete with the BRI. However, uncertainties

---

[46] On 12 November 2018 the Australia's Department of Foreign Affairs and Trade (DFAT) and Export Finance and Insurance Corporation (Efic), the Japan Bank for International Cooperation (JBIC), and the US Overseas Private Investment Corporation (OPIC) signed a Trilateral Memorandum of Understanding (MOU) to operationalize the Trilateral Partnership for Infrastructure Investment in the Indo-Pacific announced in Washington, DC, on 30 July. Their stated intention is to work together to mobilize and support the deployment of private sector investment capital to deliver major new infrastructure projects, enhance digital connectivity and energy infrastructure, and achieve mutual development goals in the Indo-Pacific.

remain about how this will work and how the reluctant private sector can be brought into the game.

Also, in December 2018, the Asia Reassurance Act (ARIA) was passed with a budget of US$1.5 billion annually over five years for the Indo-Pacific, a significant amount of which is likely earmarked for Southeast Asia. It calls for closer US engagement with ASEAN and support for ASEAN centrality. It also calls upon the president to negotiate economic and strategic engagement frameworks with ASEAN and to report annually to Congress on the implementation. ARIA further requires the US administration to push Southeast Asian states to improve human rights, democracy and good governance and to support the July 2016 ruling of the Permanent Court of Arbitration on the Philippines case against China's expansive claims in the SCS. These are touchy subjects in parts of Southeast Asia and the US administration would be well advised to broach them with sensitivity, and behind closed doors. Their utility should be viewed in the broader context where China wins merit points by respecting the existing political systems of states.[47]

Making an Impact

Some American observers have argued that the US is already deeply and comprehensively engaged in Southeast Asia in various spheres.[48] Yet the irony is that the US is not making enough of a political impact on the region compared to China. A survey of elite attitudes in Southeast

---

[47] The US opened up new pathways for an expansion of China-Thailand cooperation, especially in the military sphere, through its actions in relation to the military coup in Thailand in 2014. The traditional Thai ruling elite saw the threat from former Premier Thaksin as an existential one needing extreme measures to neutralize. To them, the US insensitivity contrasted sharply with China's assurances that it would not interfere in the domestic politics of Thailand. The political cultures and institutions needed for the healthy functioning of democracy may take a long time to evolve in societies with long-established authoritarian traditions.

[48] See, for example, David Shambaugh, *US Relations with Southeast Asia in 2018: More Continuity than Change*, Trends in Southeast Asia, no. 18/2018 (Singapore: ISEAS – Yusof Ishak Institute, 2018).

Asia done by the ISEAS – Yusof Ishak Institute at the beginning of 2019 demonstrates this. When asked which country has the most political and strategic influence in Southeast Asia, 45.2 per cent of the respondents cited China, while 30.5 per cent ranked the US ahead. The response to economic influence was even more striking: 73 per cent said China had the most economic influence while only 7.9 per cent said the US, and 6.2 per cent chose Japan and 1.7 per cent the EU.[49] This was way out of proportion to the facts on the ground: While China is the largest trading partner of Southeast Asia, the US is by far the largest investor and also a substantial trading partner. And both the EU and Japan are bigger investors than China in Southeast Asia, and major trading partners with the region.[50]

As a result of this reputational "influence deficit", the US government is becoming aware of the need to step up its public diplomacy in Southeast Asia. David Shambaugh points out that the extensive US presence is not well appreciated or reported by regional media, whereas China's presence and influence is pervasive: "Most Southeast Asian governments are often reluctant to recognize or publicize the U.S. presence or contributions to regional security, stability, and growth." He said that:

> The United States maintains a comprehensive and robust presence throughout Southeast Asia that has grown dramatically since the 1980s. It includes the commercial, security, education and diplomatic, and other domains. America's strengths and contributions to the region lie particularly in both hard and soft power, but the U.S. economic footprint is both broad and deep.

Washington is likely to address this shortcoming by stepping up its public diplomacy to better promote its narrative in Southeast Asia. An important agency for this task will be the Global Engagement Centre in the State Department that has dedicated funds for the purpose.

---

[49] "The State of Southeast Asia: 2019 Survey Report", ISEAS – Yusof Ishak Institute, Singapore, 29 January 2019.
[50] Ibid.

Public diplomacy, while important, may not suffice however to bridge the US "influence deficit" in Southeast Asia. Southeast Asian countries are being drawn into China's orbit not because they trust or like China (indeed the same ISEAS survey showed that China is the least trusted among the major countries) but because they regard the economic cost of opposing China's agenda as being too high. The message that China will use economic punishment against countries perceived to be unwilling to accommodate its interests has been driven home by past acts of such punishment in Asia and elsewhere.[51] China has also skilfully managed to create the impression that the expansion of its power and influence in the region is unstoppable. Its expansion and militarization in the SCS without any real opposition from the Obama administration; the negative image of the US resulting from the governance style and conduct of President Trump and his perceived pro-Israel policies (nearly half the population of Southeast Asia is Muslim) are among the important factors that have contributed to the relative decline of US influence. China has also stepped up its penetration of the region, including through powerful organizations like the Chinese Communist Party's United Front Work Department, International Department (formerly known as the International Liaison Department) and Publicity Department (the new incarnation of Propaganda Department). Beijing seems much better organized than Washington to influence opinion in Southeast Asia. Nothing less than a sustained long-term US engagement, together with its allies and with the requisite public diplomacy, can help to restore US credibility vis-à-vis what is seen as a consistent, growing and long-term Chinese presence. Many in Southeast Asia are still sceptical of US ability to do likewise.

It is true that Southeast Asians have always complained about lack of US attention to Southeast Asia. They are not happy when the US

---

[51] Examples in Asia include cessation of imports of bananas from the Philippines, boycott of Japanese businesses and of Korean goods in retaliation for acts by these countries deemed as unfriendly to China. Tourists from China make an important contribution to the economies of a number of Asian states. Turning off and on the tourist tap to alternate pain and relief serves not only as an economic weapon but also a psychological one.

president does not turn up for ASEAN summits. They forget, though, that the US is a global power, much more so than China, and it has global responsibilities. Often there are crises in some part of the world or other which demand priority attention from the American president. China, on the other hand, is still more of a regional power, and Southeast Asia, which it sees as part of its neighbourhood, would naturally merit more attention. So until recently, it could perhaps be said that Southeast Asians were overly sensitive in their perceived neglect by the US. But now that Southeast Asia is becoming a centre of intensified high-stakes rivalry with China, "showing up" at the appropriate level has become a necessity for the US since that, in Asian political culture, matters greatly.

What do the Americans expect from Southeast Asia? At least privately, many Southeast Asian officials express support for a continued American security presence in the region. In discussions in Washington, a number of interviewees mentioned that one thing the US needs is more access for its military forces. Though they did not say so, this could be because access to Philippine bases and facilities has become uncertain under the Duterte administration. Such access would help to maintain some balance of power in the region. Yet hardly any Southeast Asian country is prepared to provide more access for the US military—for fear of offending China.

Public statements of support would be most welcome by the Americans but these have become fewer or weaker in recent years. In part for reasons of domestic public support, traditionally the US likes to rationalize its foreign deployments and wars in terms of helping local friends who face aggression or bullying. On the South China Sea issue there is not enough open regional support. Marvin Ott says that even symbolic backing would help. As an example of symbolic support, he floated the idea of allowing US Navy sailors from US warships to do sunbathing or scuba diving on one of the islands occupied by countries other than China. The photos of such recreation would be splashed on media in the US and show the American public local understanding for their sailors' endeavours in the South China Sea. However, no Southeast Asian claimant state would be prepared to allow this.[52]

---

[52] Conversation with Marvin C. Ott, 16 May 2019.

Other suggestions made by some Americans interviewees were: Southeast Asia countries should enhance the attractiveness of the region to foreign investors by making the necessary domestic reforms; and have a more open and objective discussion in the media and academic circles of the region on the value and shortcomings of the Chinese BRI.

The South China Sea

The SCS is viewed in Washington not as a "Southeast Asian" issue, but as a maritime theatre for the wider contest against China over who controls the western Pacific. This contrasts with the perception sometimes encountered in Southeast Asia that the SCS is already "lost" to China. This idea surprised my interviewees. For example, Dan Blumenthal said flatly: "The US is not giving up on the South China Sea."[53] In the US, the SCS is viewed very much as a contested sea in the context of the new tougher policy towards China. Freedom of Navigation Operations (FNOPS) have increased significantly under the Trump administration, and the US has also multilateralized the problem by getting other outside powers like the UK, France, Japan and Australia to send their naval ships into the SCS.[54]

Will the US go to war in the SCS if China attacks a US ship or plane? The interviewees felt that China is very unlikely to do this because it does not yet have the confidence that it can win such a conflict. Will the American public support a conflict with China in the SCS? Would Trump do so? One of my interviewees thought that the American public does not know how important the SCS is and may not want the US to go to war over it.

However, Marvin Ott has a different view: According to him:

> The South China Sea is now a core interest of the US. Indeed, it is the most likely place where the confrontation between the rising

---

[53] Interview with Dan Blumenthal, Director of Asian Studies, American Enterprise Institute, 16 May 2019.

[54] From interviews with David Shambaugh (29 April 2019), Robert Sutter (7 May 2019), Bonnie Glaser (9 May 2019), and Dan Blumenthal (16 May 2019).

power and the established one will take place, if and when it does. Perhaps Trump does not care much about the South China Sea, but he can easily be persuaded by showing how the sea fits into China's strategy against the US. In particular, if a US ship or plane is attacked by China, it is very likely that Trump will not back down. The US is greatly outnumbered in the South China Sea by the Chinese navy in terms of surface ships, even though US ships are qualitatively superior. However, the US has a lead in undersea warfare. China would not want to risk a confrontation. Will the American public support the administration in a conflict in the South China Sea? If a US ship is sunk (or if China attacks Taiwan) the US will fight even if China has local military superiority. It is in the "DNA" of the US to do so, even if it loses the initial battle before concentrating forces from other parts of the world and throwing in everything it has. Public opinion in the US will shift immediately once the media blare out a Chinese attack on a US navy ship or aircraft. This is something that Southeast Asian countries may not realize, but China probably does.[55]

PERCEPTIONS AND MISPERCEPTIONS

There is a tendency in parts of Southeast Asia to be overly pessimistic about the US and overly bullish about China. This is due in part to a poor understanding of the US and also to excessive confidence in the idea that a present perceived trend will continue into the longer-term future when the future remains essentially unpredictable.

How Dysfunctional and Distracted Is the US?

There is often a lack of understanding of how the US political system works. Some are inclined to think that American politics and governance today are so chaotic and unworkable that the US can be written off as a global superpower and as a major factor in Asian geopolitics. Such a

---

[55] Interview with Marvin Ott, 16 May 2019.

pessimistic reading is influenced in part by the more than usual disorder in US domestic politics and the crude and erratic behaviour of President Trump. Media organizations in a democratic society tend to give prominence to such developments.

The US political system is however in reality more complex than that of many other democracies. The separation of powers in the US between the executive, Congress and the judiciary at different levels of government from federal to state and so on has always had some appearance of disorder. The divisiveness has seemed more pronounced in recent years because of the polarization between the two political parties, and Trump's presidency has accentuated the apparent chaos.

Yet, there are important continuities. Even as Trump castigates allies and multilateral organizations, his officials continue to underline the importance of alliances. There is widespread recognition within the Trump administration of the importance of Southeast Asia in America's contest with China. The very fact that the US has decided to check China's ambitions in Asia and the determination with which it is moving in that direction show that it will remain a major factor in Asia.[56] This is irrespective of whether Trump wins or loses the 2020 presidential election. Post-Trump, there will probably be some return to the pre-Trump respect for alliances and partnerships, as the US seeks to rebuild a broad coalition to constrain China.

The US is turning around from nearly half a century of engagement with China to a likely long period ahead of strategic competition, possibly even a new Cold War. This turnaround has just started and will take time to complete.[57] Such big changes in direction always tend to be messy,

---

[56] Witness, for example, the haste with which it is deploying mobile land-based conventional intermediate range ballistic missiles in the western Pacific to counter similar weapons which China has deployed for years targeting Taiwan and US bases in the western Pacific.

[57] Conversation with a retired defence official who is involved in turning around government departments for this purpose.

especially in the initial stages. The US can be inconsistent, sometimes with costly consequences.[58] It can be erratic and initially make mistakes when confronted with a major new challenge, but it can be a potent force after it has organized itself for the task ahead.

A proper understanding of American politics may also be hampered by a certain political conditioning in several Southeast Asian countries. Some regional governments regard liberal democracy as unsuited for their circumstances, and instead place a high premium on stability and cohesion. However, the political values of stability and community solidarity articulated over the decades by politicians and the regional mass media cannot be without influence on the thinking of at least sections of the populations, which may also align with messages coming from China in recent years extolling the stability of its authoritarian system compared to the instability of the American democracy.

A related argument is that the US is "unreliable" because it abandons allies and partners as it did South Vietnam in the 1970s and the Kurds today. The US is indeed looking more "unreliable" these days because it is reappraising its policies which is causing much uncertainty. And it may also be more prone to changes in policy because it is a democracy in which public opinion and competitive elections have greater bearing on foreign policy than is the case in authoritarian states. President Trump's behaviour only heightens this perception of American "unreliability".

However, being "unreliable" is not unique to the US or intrinsically part of the American character. Great powers change their policy course when it is seen to be failing, as the Soviet Union did in 1988–89 when it "abandoned" to the mercy of the Taliban the pro-Soviet Najibullah regime in Kabul. It also "abandoned" several Warsaw Pact regimes that had also

---

[58] In the late 1940s, then Secretary of State Dean Acheson declared that the Korean peninsula lay outside the US "defence perimeter", thereby inadvertently giving a green light to North Korea to invade the South in 1950, only to face US military intervention to resist the invasion. In 1990 the US Ambassador in Baghdad told Iraqi President Saddam Hussein that the US had no interest in inter-Arab quarrels and conflicts, which may have led Saddam Hussein to think that the US would not intervene when he invaded Kuwait—but the US did intervene.

depended on its support for survival and Vietnam in Southeast Asia. China may seem "reliable" today but only because after two centuries of weakness, it is still in the early stages of expanding its overseas reach and commitments.

Some allude to America's socio-economic problems—the increased inequalities in American society and stagnant wages for the bottom half of the population for many years.[59] These are certainly a cause for concern. Democracies, more than other systems of government, rely on public support for the nature and the extent of their engagement with the external world. Globalization damaged the manufacturing industries in America—shutting down factories in the rust belt and hollowing out towns with severe economic and social consequences for the people. No sound policies were taken to mitigate these effects.

While these developments are of concern and hold implications for foreign policy, their amelioration could take place over time. It is premature to regard them as foreshadowing the end of the US as a global superpower. That may happen some day or it may not. It is worth remembering that the US has always shown a great capacity for regeneration. Whichever the case, the economy is doing well at present, and unemployment is low and wages have risen.[60]

Has Power Shifted in Favour of China?

While a significant power shift has indeed been underway, its effects should not be exaggerated. China faces a number of serious problems such as an ageing population, environmental degradation, high debt and financial imbalances, a slowing economic growth rate, industrial overcapacity, and other serious challenges. Now, it is also losing some of its export markets.

---

[59] Danny Quah, Dean, Lee Kuan Yew School of Public Policy, National University of Singapore. "The US is, indeed, the exceptional nation: Income dynamics in the bottom 50%" (Jan 2019), ResearchGate DOI: 10.13140/RG.2.2.23376.97289.

[60] According to the US Bureau of Labor Statistics, the unemployment rate fell to 3.5 per cent in September 2019, a 50-year low.

China's GDP is going to exceed that of the US not because the country is more advanced in a comprehensive way, but because its population is more than four times larger. According to the World Bank, China's GDP per capita in 2018 was US$9,771, which was a little bit lower than that for Malaysia which stood at US$11,239. Both rank in the middle-income category. The US figure for the same year was US$62,641.

We know that South Korea and Taiwan easily and impressively broke out of the middle-income trap and became rich countries. Will China follow suit, quickly becoming a country three or four times more powerful economically than the US, with all the strategic implications that would entail? Many scholars of China are sceptical.[61] For example, the late Professor John Wong of Singapore's East Asia Institute expected China to escape the middle-income trap (MIT) but was still not too sanguine about the future of the Chinese economy. In an article published in 2016, three years before the start of the US-China trade war, Wong said:

> If the MIT was not really its hurdle, China's major challenges would soon surface once it has crossed the threshold of a developed economy. With its huge population, China would face an enormous task of further raising its per capita income to become a truly affluent society that is characteristic of many developed economies of the West and Japan. China could run into the risk of falling into a new kind of trap, the "low-income developed-economy trap".[62]

---

[61] See, for example, David Shambaugh, *China's Future* (Cambridge: Polity Press, 2016).

[62] See John Wong "China and the Middle Income Trap", *East Asia Policy* 8, no. 3 (2016). See also the new book *China's Invisible Crisis: How a Growing Urban-Rural Divide Could Sink the World's Second Largest Economy*, by Scott Rozelle who argues after extensive research that serious deficiencies in education for the new technological era outside China's big cities and especially in the rural areas could make China's transition from middle income difficult.

As Ashley Tellis put it: "The question is not just whether China can overtake the US, it is whether it can sustain the overtaking."[63]

Still, there is no denying that the sheer economic mass of China, irrespective of whether it outstrips the US or not, will have a huge impact on neighbouring countries.

China is also a society that is ageing before it has become rich. There were 11 per cent fewer births in 2018 than in 2017, and births in 2017 were lower than in 2016—despite the easing and then the abolition of the one-child policy. Meanwhile, life expectancy has increased. Based on China's official statistics and other data, by 2030, people who are 60 years and older will account for more than a quarter of the population. This will require much more government expenditure on social services to care for the aged and to meet rising expectations of the population, according to Wang Feng and Yong Cai.[64] Furthermore, China's massive current account surpluses are disappearing and it will not have the seemingly unlimited resources for the military as it had in the past. The defence budget is presently still increasing by about 7 per cent a year.

In terms of military power, China has significantly narrowed the military gap with the US—but it has not bridged it. Its anti-access strategy has made it more costly for the US to fight China in the vicinity of Taiwan or in the SCS. However, the US is now gearing up to maintain its lead with increases in its military budget. Marvin Ott again:

> George Kennan years ago observed that Americans tend to be slow in recognizing threats and committing forces to deal with them. But once the process starts it becomes a massive effort with few restraints. I think we are seeing something like this occurring with regard to China's strategic reach into the South China Sea and Western Pacific. Since the 9/11 attacks the US, collectively,

---

[63] Interview with Ashley Tellis, 24 April 2019.

[64] Wang Feng is professor of sociology at the University of California, Irvine. Yong Cai is associate professor of sociology and a fellow at the Carolina Population Centre, University of North Carolina at Chapel Hill.

has been preoccupied with perceived challenges in the Middle East and southwest Asia. But now the switch has been thrown and attention is shifting to China's maritime power play. Over the next few years, we will see a very large commitment to upgrade and strengthen the American military presence in that arena. The current balance of power is temporary and the future trajectory highly dynamic.[65]

China's military modernization still has a considerable way to go before it can reach US levels.[66]

The United States possesses three other major military advantages. First, it has a network of worldwide military bases or facilities with other countries. China is only now searching for overseas bases and facilities. The first one is at Djibouti in the Indian Ocean near the Horn of Africa. Second, the US has significant allies and partners in the Indo-Pacific region which can add to its weight, the most important being Japan, Australia and India. It can also rope in others like Britain, France and Canada. China has no ally in Asia, except perhaps Pakistan which does not have a significant navy, though it has struck a close military relationship with Russia and has benefitted from Russian military technology and other support. Third, US armed forces have operational combat experience which the People's Liberation Army (PLA) does not have. The prospects of China soon dominating high-tech industries and with that outclassing the US military are highly uncertain.

The US has many ways of making life uncomfortable for China even without the use of force—through economic and financial means, for example, given the status of the US dollar in international transactions. Also, a glance at the map will show that China is surrounded by states that do not trust it, opening up possibilities for the US in the event of a new Cold War.

---

[65] Marvin Ott, in e-mail communication, 29 September 2019.
[66] Conversation with Dr Tim Huxley, Executive Director, International Institute of Strategic Studies (IISS)-Asia.

CONCLUSION

Trump's coming may have been a necessary, if jolting, reminder of the need to address America's strategic overreach and unresolved domestic socio-economic issues. It has also made America aware of the challenge from China and the need to respond to it firmly.

However, Trump's unilateralism, capriciousness and shabby treatment of allies and friends have damaged US interests and reputation abroad, and in Southeast Asia may be accelerating the shift towards China. They are also contributing to the great uncertainty that policymakers and political analysts everywhere are trying to grapple with.

The current US administration's approach to China is strikingly hawkish. It sees the past "engagement" and "cooperation" with China as a fatal embrace which enabled China to exploit US openness to steal US commercial and military secrets and advanced technology through an extensive penetration of US society and unfair business practices—which has enabled it to close in on America's lead in high technology and its military pre-eminence. They may not be entirely wrong in this assessment. However, as has been argued earlier in this paper, how to disengage ("decouple") and how far to take disengagement is a complex exercise that needs to be conducted with great wisdom and care.

After Trump, US vital interests in Asia will remain what they have been for more than a century: that Asia remains open to commerce for all nations, with no closed spheres of influence. Though America's relative strategic and economic power has declined, it will still remain a powerful actor in Asia and, together with its allies, be capable of balancing China. It can be expected to move towards a balance-of-power strategy to preserve its interests, a strategy successfully employed for many years before World War II.

America post-Trump will feel different without Trump's histrionics and unpredictability. But it is unlikely to return entirely to the pre-Trump America—generous, and pursuing enlightened self-interest that also benefits others—because resources are likely to be limited and the security challenges in the Indo-Pacific region more acute.

Given the vast geographical area of the Indo-Pacific and the presence of other actors like Japan, India, Australia and ASEAN, over the longer term, neither the US nor China are likely to have dominance, and a rough balance of power is more likely to emerge there. However, it is uncertain if a balance will be attainable in the whole of Southeast Asia because of China's advantages in areas closer to it. It is still not clear whether the US will be prepared to commit the necessary resources to counteract China's influence in Southeast Asia in a comprehensive way. Much will depend on the political decisions in Washington, the resources available and how much support it gets from allies and partners.

A balance of power will be good for Southeast Asian states as it will help to preserve their sovereignty and independence, which in turn should be an important US strategic interest. Hopefully one day, China will also accept it instead of wanting to replace the waning US dominance with its own.

The US is nowhere near a terminal end as a superpower, despite Trump and problems at home; nor is China on an inevitable path of dominance of the region given its own significant domestic political and socio-economic challenges. Simply put, US receding may not be inevitable, but neither is China's dominance.